What
Discipleship?

Basics of the Faith

How Do We Glorify God?
How Our Children Come to Faith
What Are Election and Predestination?
What Are Spiritual Gifts?
What Is a Reformed Church?
What Is a True Calvinist?
What Is Biblical Preaching?
What Is Church Government?
What Is Discipleship?
What Is Grace?
What Is Hell?
What Is Justification by Faith Alone?
What Is Man?
What Is Perseverance of the Saints?
What Is Providence?
What Is Spiritual Warfare?
What Is the Atonement?
What Is the Christian Worldview?
What Is the Lord's Supper?
What Is True Conversion?
What Is Vocation?
What Is Worship Music?
Why Believe in God?
Why Do We Baptize Infants?

What Is Discipleship?

Stephen Smallman

P&R
PUBLISHING
P.O. BOX 817 • PHILLIPSBURG • NEW JERSEY 08865-0817

Page design by Tobias Design

Printed in the United States of America

Library of Congress Cataloging-in-Publication Data

Smallman, Stephen, 1940-
  What is discipleship? / Stephen Smallman.
    p. cm. -- (Basics of the faith)
  Includes bibliographical references.
  ISBN 978-1-59638-235-0 (pbk.)
  1. Discipling (Christianity) I. Title.
  BV4520.S527 2011
  248.4--dc22
                    2010054591

◻ "What is Discipleship?"

I have tried to envision who would look over a church or conference book table or scan an online catalogue and choose to read this title. Two possibilities come to mind: (1) You are a person who knows you need to be more conscientious about following Jesus but aren't sure where to start, or (2) you are a church leader who is aware of the proliferation of material available on discipleship and think that an introductory booklet will help you get into this topic. Perhaps you are particularly drawn to the fact that it is part of the Basics of the Faith series. You wonder if there is a distinctly Reformed approach to the biblical challenge to go and make disciples.

I am directing this booklet primarily to those in the second group—leaders who are asking this question in terms of what is happening in your churches. I have previously written an introduction to discipleship for people with little background in the Faith, and those who want something of a new beginning (*The Walk: Steps for New and Renewed Followers of Jesus*, P&R Publishing, 2009). Those of you who are thinking about discipleship personally will want to look at *The Walk*. However, as you read the book you will quickly discover that I don't think we can grow as disciples without the church, so I hope you will find these thoughts helpful as I direct my words to leaders in your church.

The writing of *The Walk* has given me an opportunity to think more about the larger issues affecting how our churches approach discipleship. Motivational books and disciple-ship materials are available in abundance.[1] However, there must first be a readiness by the leaders of the church to rank disciple-making as a high priority and to build the ministry of their congregations accordingly. I believe that the theology of the Reformation helps significantly to understand how we should fulfill that mandate, and I will occasionally identify what is specifically "Reformed." But our Reformed theology and practice should contribute to the larger church and her wrestling with discipleship, so what follows is a biblical answer to the question, what is discipleship?

THE CHALLENGE

Church members and leaders who commit to letting Scripture determine the priorities of the church (and that should be all of us) need go no further than a thoughtful consideration of Matthew 28:18–20, a passage known appropriately as "The Great Commission."

And Jesus came and said to them, "All authority in heaven and on earth has been given to me. Go therefore and make disciples of all nations, baptizing them in the name of the Father and of the Son and of the Holy Spirit, teaching them to observe all that I have commanded you. And behold, I am with you always, to the end of the age."

The studies of this passage I have checked point out that grammatically there is only one command—to make disci-ples. The other three key words—*go*, *baptizing*, and *teaching*—

explain what is involved in the mandate to make disciples. *Make disciples* is the verb form of the word *disciple*. Literally the command is "disciple all the nations," but the common translation, "make disciples," calls attention to the process and is an accurate translation. The KJV translated the word *teach*, which has led to some misunderstandings about the exact nature of Jesus' commission. Discipleship is more than teaching; it has the sense of following the teacher both as a learner and as an adherent.

Go, or *going*, reinforces that fact that this must be our essential task as Christians. If we are to be obedient to the commission of our risen Lord we must be *intentional* about making disciples. There are certainly missionary implications, but the mandate itself doesn't require that we physically go anywhere. The phrase *all nations* means all people (*ethne*, from which we get "ethnic"), not necessarily nations as we use the word today.

The next two key words, *baptizing* and *teaching*, are the two basic phases of making disciples. Therefore, to make disciples we first help people come to the point of baptism, which means publicly confessing Christ and becoming part of his church. This phase of making disciples is traditionally thought of as *evangelism*. Then we guide the new believer in a path of following Jesus in obedience, which has traditionally been called *discipleship*. Clearly, a *continuum* of evangelism and discipleship is the essence of "making disciples" and must be fundamental if we are to understand and implement the Great Commission.

When we consider that Jesus began the Great Commission with a statement of his authority and ended it with an absolute promise of his ongoing presence as this great work is undertaken, we can properly conclude that making disciples of the nations is a work that Jesus himself is doing through his church. Can there be any question then that this is Jesus' first priority for the work of his church?

A recent expression of this challenge has been issued by Christian brethren from Australia. In their book, *The Trellis and the Vine*, the authors write, "The commission is not fundamentally about mission out there somewhere else in another country. *It's a commission that makes disciple-making the normal agenda and priority of every church and every Christian disciple.* . . . Thus the goal of Christian ministry is quite simple, and in a sense measurable: are we making and nurturing genuine disciples of Christ?"[2]

The image of the trellis and the vine is quite striking. The authors point out that for a church, a "trellis" (committees, organization, buildings, and other physical infrastructure) is important only as it serves as a stable platform for the vine to grow on. Growth of the vine is making disciples—"to see people converted, changed and grow to maturity in the gospel."[3] Sadly, we tend to give so much attention to constructing a good trellis that there is little time to give attention to the purpose of the trellis—the growing up of a strong vine. In fact the general pattern in our churches is that "trellis work" tends to take over "vine work."[4]

Another pastor expresses the same idea by stating that typically churches settle for becoming "ABC churches"—those concerned with attendance, building, and cash.

> The ABC church is alive and well in the United States—if we can bring ourselves to use the words, "alive" and "well." It's safe to say that a large majority of Protestant congregations have made attendance, building, and cash—as opposed to Christ's Great Commission in Matthew 28:18–20 to be and to make disciples—their organizational bottom line.[5]

The real bottom line when we look at the Great Commission is to build up a church that views itself as a community of disciples of Jesus who are making disciples, even as they grow in their own discipleship. The challenge of the Great Commission raises some very significant and possibly disturbing questions.

- How much attention do I give "making disciples" in my own life and ministry?
- How seriously does our church take the clear mandate of the Great Commission?
- Is there concrete evidence that we are making disciples, both in terms of introducing people to Jesus and in teaching them to walk along the path he has set before them?

KEY BUILDING BLOCKS IN RESPONDING TO THE CHALLENGE OF MATTHEW 28

An adequate response to this great challenge will take you well beyond what I'm writing in this booklet, which is why it ends with a section called "Next Steps." The following are some first considerations for prayerfully envisioning "making disciples" in your church or ministry. These are ten basic foundation blocks for building a church that is seriously committed to making disciples. The list is by no means complete, but I hope it stimulates movement toward the mission of our Lord.

1. Every true believer must think of himself or herself as a disciple of Jesus.

Somehow the idea that being a disciple of Jesus is not an essential aspect of salvation, but is instead an extra step or deeper commitment, has been allowed to take root in the consciousness of many Christians. This kind of thinking has led to identifying discipleship with programs that are intended for those believers who are interested and willing to move forward in their walk of faith. As a consequence discipleship is regarded as optional—important to be sure, but not essential to salvation.

James Montgomery Boice began his book, *Christ's Call to Discipleship*, with the following,

> But I say at the outset that the arguments of the following chapters are essentially one thesis, namely that discipleship is not a supposed second step in Christianity as if one first becomes a believer in Jesus and then, if he chooses, a disciple. From the beginning discipleship is involved in what it means to be a Christian.[6]

Reading about the "disciples" in the gospel accounts can raise some questions because it is not always clear if Jesus is speaking of disciples in general or those twelve disciples he called and set apart as apostles. However, any confusion should be cleared away by reading Acts where *disciple* becomes the usual word for believers or brothers or the church (6:1–2, 7; 9:1, 10, 19, 26–31). A key text in this regard is Acts 11:26: "In Antioch the disciples were first called Christians." This is the post-resurrection understanding of a disciple, and in our churches *all* who profess to be believers in Jesus should embrace the truth that discipleship pertains to them. No doubt we will need to confess that we are weak disciples or new disciples or struggling disciples—but it is vital that believers understand that *they are disciples*. Owning that truth is a key step to a more productive discipleship.

Those who are pastors and teachers in Christ's church should let this truth sink deeply into their consciousness so that it impacts their preaching. One reason Christians make discipleship an added commitment is that they have only heard the gospel as a call to believe in Jesus for forgiveness and salvation, not as a call to follow Jesus. We need to preach a gospel that *assumes* discipleship because to believe in Jesus is to follow Jesus as his disciple. Before we fault the members of our churches for their weakness in this area, we need to ask ourselves what is the content of the gospel message we have been consistently proclaiming.

2. The life of a disciple of Jesus begins with the call of Jesus.

In the story of the earliest call to discipleship, Mark tells us that Jesus appeared on the scene taking up his public ministry by preaching repentance and faith in the good news. He then called four fishermen to follow him—which they did immediately (Mark 1:14–20). In the next chapter he called Levi to leave behind his tax collecting business and follow him—which Levi did.[7] Later that day Jesus spoke of what he was doing in terms of the call: "I came not to *call* the righteous, but sinners" (2:13–17). Based on these passages, and consistent with other Scripture, I define a disciple of Jesus as a person who has *heard the call of Jesus* and has responded by *repenting, believing the gospel,* and *following him.*[8]

The ability to hear the call of Jesus introduces the important question of how a sinner, described as "dead in the trespasses and sins" (Eph. 2:1–3), can actually hear Jesus' call. The gospel accounts describe the human response to that call, but in the greater context of the New Testament it is clear that hearing the call of Jesus requires a supernatural work of God—what is typically defined as regeneration or effectual calling.[9] For example, in describing the conversion of Lydia, we read, "the Lord opened her heart to pay attention to what was said by Paul" (Acts 16:14). The Westminster Shorter catechism defines this specifically as a "work of the Holy Spirit" that enables us to "embrace Jesus Christ freely offered to us in the gospel."[10] We distinguish between a *gospel call*, where Christ is proclaimed to all and his *effectual call*, where God works in the heart to bring about transformation. In I Corinthians 1:18–24 Paul explained that the gospel is "a stumbling block to Jews and folly to Gentiles, but to those who are *called*," the same message is, "the power of God and the wisdom of God."

We should not think of the call to salvation in Christ and the call to discipleship as different. They are simply two ways to understand the same supernatural work of effectual calling. It is difficult for many teachers and leaders in the church to emphasize following Jesus in their presentation of the gospel because they assume that discipleship begins after a person's decision to believe. They are so passionate to avoid any suggestion that salvation is a result of human works that anything calling for effort other than a faith commitment or "decision for Jesus" is studiously avoided. Well-meaning evangelists will even speak of how *easy* it is to become a Christian. Any thought of "take up your cross and follow me" (Mark 8:34) is a matter to be considered *after* responding to the gospel. However, once we understand that people come to Christ because of the supernatural call, we will also understand that ultimately what is drawing them is Jesus working through the Holy Spirit. Therefore, the reality that this new life will not be easy (as Jesus made clear in his gospel preaching) will not keep those being called from believing.

Practically this also means that we shouldn't need to coax Christians into being interested in being disciples. A life of following Jesus proceeds naturally from one who has been born into the family of God, and it should be presented as such. Those who are not interested in living as a disciple should be challenged to examine their hearts and ask themselves whether they have actually met Christ as Lord and Savior.

This is one of the key ways in which Reformed theology should inform our approach to discipleship. In most of the discipleship literature I have read, there are only occasional references to the work of the Holy Spirit and the need for regeneration. An author may even insist that regeneration is foundational for any consideration of discipleship, but then nothing more is said. It is as though there is a nod to solid theology, but then a rush to get to practical issues. However, the work of the Holy Spirit and God's call is a practical as well as theological issue. It is the enabling power of the Holy Spirit that brings us into the new life, and it is the power of the Holy Spirit that enables us to walk in the new life. Paul said, "If we live by the Spirit, let us also walk by the Spirit" (Gal. 5:25). Our role in making disciples needs to be understood in terms of how we work as instruments of what the Holy Spirit is doing in the lives of people. Several years ago a popular book on disciple-ship had as its title a phrase that has been quoted frequently in subsequent literature: *Disciples are Made not Born.* [11] I would respectfully disagree and say, "disciples must be born (again) before they can be made."

3. Discipleship is not a distinct category or activity, but a synonym for Christian living.

Although this point may be clear from what has been said, it is important to keep this truth before us regularly because there is a constant temptation to confine discipleship to particular programs or groups. Discipleship then becomes one of many activities of the church when, in fact, "making disciples" needs to define the essential mission of the church.

One way to think of discipleship is to consider it as the human response to the work of the Spirit in sanctification. God is forming his people into the image of Christ, and helping those people live out what God is doing within them is discipleship. For example, read Colossians 3:5–17 as an agenda for discipling oth-ers as well as a personal challenge for your own discipleship.

Within this broader understanding of discipleship, it is certainly appropriate to have special seasons of study or specific programs designed to help people with their walk with Christ. An example of this came from a class I taught recently called "Making Disciples." One of the members grasped the core idea and realized that the men's ministry he was leading in his church was essentially meeting simply because that is what they had been doing for years. With prayer, work, and consultation with his pastor, he redesigned the ministry to teach men what he was learning about a man's walk with Christ. He set it up so that those men learned by teaching others. These were disciples growing as disciples by making disciples.

However, along with specific ministries that might be labeled discipleship, there needs to be a general consciousness that everything in the church should be viewed through the lens of making disciples. For example, if your church has a choir (or choirs) or a worship team, what is going on within them that contributes to the members' spiritual growth? And in the context of the whole congregation, do these groups appreciate how worship is a critical component of the life of following Jesus as a community? Are small groups viewed as centers of disciple-making? What about women's ministries or the work of deacons?

4. The Great Commission does not make our modern distinction between evangelism and discipleship.

This point has already been made in our study of the Great Commission (Matt. 28:18–20) earlier in this booklet. Our risen Savior and King sent out his disciples to make disciples of the nations (the unbelievers all around them), but the goal was not simply conversion or obtaining what are termed "decisions for Jesus." The goal was to "make disciples," which meant leading those who profess faith and are baptized into a

14

life of following Jesus. Unfortunately, this is not the way many churches view ministry.

In some larger churches, for example, evangelism and discipleship can be two different departments of ministry operating somewhat independently from each other. Pastors often think in terms of a "salvation message" *vs.* a "discipleship message," and they can be quite different messages. This approach is another reason why our churches are full of those who profess to be Christians but don't take the matter of discipleship seriously.

One very helpful resource is the writing of Dr. Robert Webber in his series of books called Ancient-Future. In *Ancient-Future Evangelism: Making Your Church a Faith-Forming Community*,[12] the author explains the practice of the early church and how it approached evangelism, discipleship, and spiritual formation as a *unified* ministry. Thus, he claims, the ancient church should inform the future church and lead us to a more biblical understanding of making disciples in the local church. We can't duplicate the early church, and Webber doesn't advocate that, but there are some very important lessons to be learned about the continuum of evangelism and discipleship from our fathers in the faith.

As a practical application of this unity of mission, start to think in terms of two phases of making disciples rather than distinct tasks of evangelism and discipleship. In fact, if many of us stop and reflect on how we were "evangelized," it could be better described as being discipled in the context of a loving family or community of believers until we publicly confessed trust in the gospel we had seen lived out in others. We must ask ourselves what is needed to make our congregations places where this kind of evangelism is a normal part of the life of the church. Do we authentically welcome unbelievers to come among us and take whatever time is necessary to seek and find Christ? Are we prepared to lead them step-by-step from initial profession of faith into a life of maturity in Christ? As implications of these questions filter into the life of a congregation, they will lower the invisible "walls" and create a more welcoming environment.

5. The gospel is what is most needed by believers as well as unbelievers.

There has been a reawakening to the fact that the gospel, the announcement of God's deliverance through Jesus Christ, is more than a message for those who have not yet believed it. One expression of that reawakening is the statement, I need to preach the gospel to myself every day.[13] The more common pattern has been to equate preaching the gospel with evangelism, but once someone has believed the gospel we are not sure how to describe what comes next. Jerry Bridges explains it this way: "What one word describes the Bible message you most needed to hear as an unbeliever? I suggest the word is the *gospel*. . . . What one word describes the message we most need to hear as believers? I get a lot of different answers to that question, but most of them can be summed up with one word, *discipleship*." He goes on to explain that, in fact, the word a believer must continue to hear in order to be an effective disciple is *gospel*.[14] In much of our teaching and practice in churches the gospel is actually separated from discipleship when exactly the *opposite* is needed.

Archibald Alexander, one of the greatest pastors and teachers of American Presbyterianism asked why "Christians commonly are of so diminutive a stature and of such feeble strength in their religion." The primary cause, he concluded, was that believers were not being taught the sufficiency of Christ and the freeness of divine grace in salvation. "Until religious teachers inculcate clearly, fully, and practically, the grace of God as manifested in the Gospel, we shall have no vigorous growth of piety among professing Christians."[15] That was written in 1844. The challenge to disciple believers through a "depth presentation of the gospel"[16] is one that constantly needs to be restated.

One of the key texts in this awakening is a fresh look at Romans 1:16: "I am not ashamed of the gospel, for it is the power of God for salvation to everyone who believes." A study of Romans reveals clearly that "salvation" is far more than conversion—it is *all that we are given in Christ*, including justification, sanctification, adoption, and glorification. Furthermore the word *believe* in the text is in the progressive form of "is believing," pointing to ongoing faith in the gospel rather than a single experience. The gospel empowers those who believe it to live a life of following Jesus. Michael Horton states it this way: "Precisely [because] the Good News [is] of a completed, sufficient, and perfect work of God in Christ accomplished for me and outside of me in history, the gospel is 'the power of God unto salvation' not only at the beginning but throughout the Christian life. In fact, our sanctification is simply a lifelong process of letting that Good News sink in and responding appropriately: becoming the people whom God says that we already are in Christ."[17] In other words, those who have come to believe the gospel don't move on from the gospel; they need to learn how to go deeper into the gospel.

Trying to think through practically and pastorally what it actually means to apply the gospel to those who already believe was one of my major purposes in writing *The Walk*. I call it "Discipleship Through the Gospel" and outline four basic steps, suggested by Romans, for what that could look like.[18] How to disciple, whatever form it takes, must grow from a basic conviction that the gospel is the essential tool we need to make disciples.

6. Don't assume that people understand the gospel either in terms of experience or theology.

When I lead a seminar on gospel discipling I frequently ask the group, "How much of the gospel did you understand when you first believed?" The response is usually smiles and comments about how *little* they actually understood when God worked in their hearts to trust in Christ. Thankfully, we are saved by grace poured into our hearts by a merciful God, not by the depth of our understanding. By his grace we had enough awareness of our need and awareness that Jesus died for our sins to exercise feeble faith that God could rescue us. Even that faith was a gift of God as God made us new in Christ (Eph. 2:8–10).

People are at all levels of spiritual understanding in our churches. In some instances, "faith" is actually on a false foundation and not true saving faith at all. Or we may be working with saved people who nevertheless need to relearn almost everything about the gospel. Ultimately, only God truly knows the heart. The point is that as we consider how our churches will go about making disciples, we should not make assumptions about where people are in their journeys or how much of the gospel story they actually understand even when they can use familiar vocabulary. My book, *The Walk*, deliberately took what I thought of as a "discipleship for dummies" approach, and I encouraged older believers to read it in preparation for discipling others. However, many of the responses indicated that more mature believers discovered truths of the gospel that were new to them.

We want everyone in our large gatherings or small groups to be invited as a learner. It doesn't mean that we become superficial, but it does mean avoiding casual statements such as, "Of course everyone here knows the story of Elijah . . ." or announcing a text of Scripture and then not giving any time for a beginner to actually look it up because we assume that "everyone here knows their Bibles." With just a slight change of language (reflecting a significant change in attitude) we can create a church that inspires growth at every level. If leadership adopts this idea, it will also become part of the way the entire church goes about its work.

7. The teaching of gospel doctrine was fundamental to Paul's discipleship of new believers.

Typical materials that are made available for discipleship programs major on what could be called the "doing" of the Christian life. These may be personal spiritual disciplines such as prayer, Bible study, or fasting, or more active disciplines such as community service and missionary work. These are worthy things to do as followers of Jesus, but is this the place to start?

Paul approached this important question of living as disciples in another way. He taught again and again that the basis for "doing" must be "knowing."[19] The epistle of Paul to the Romans is often subtitled "The Gospel according to Paul." That is an appropriate label and therefore Romans can be viewed as Paul's outline for discipleship through the gospel. Michael Horton states, "It strikes me as significant that even when Paul wrote to well-established churches (like Rome) he began with the story." And indeed the first four verses of Romans are a restatement of the coming of Christ to fulfill God's purposes—which is the essence of the gospel story. Horton continues, "Then, without leaving the story behind, he interprets its plot through steep and breathtaking doctrinal vistas until finally he is lost in wonder and praise in the doxologies of chapters 9 and 11." It is only then that Paul becomes specific about what it means to live out what has been given to us in Christ. "Discipleship—following Christ—means being called away from our dead-end plots to become part of his story; to be taught by him so that we find ourselves entrusting our lives to him in growing confidence. Only then can discipleship be something other than a lot of busywork."[20]

Keep in mind that the most significant reality of following Christ in the gospel accounts is the presence of Christ himself.

Those first disciples were learning about who their master and leader was by actually being with him as he taught, fed the hungry, cast out demons, calmed the storm, and then died and rose from the dead. Disciples since that unique time need to give extensive attention to the challenge of knowing Christ and his presence as the basis for practically following Christ. This is what the apostle Paul was constantly praying for himself and the churches he wrote to.[21]

Horton adds a very significant observation here. An emphasis on following Christ without taking the time to know Christ and who we are in Christ tends to make the major theme of discipleship the imitation of Christ. This is a worthy activity but impossible to do in our human energy no matter how dedicated and disciplined we are. In fact, *following Christ is a consequence of our spiritual union with Christ*, which Paul explains in Romans 6–8.

> Nowhere in this lodestar passage for the Christian life does Paul direct our attention to the imitation of Christ. . . . Rather, he teaches something far greater than an example to imitate. He calls us not simply to imitate Christ but to be crucified, buried, and raised with him. . . . Paul does not say, "Be like Jesus." He says, "You *are* like Jesus. He is the head and you are part of his body; he is the first fruits and you are the rest of the harvest."[22]

If you think of theology and doctrine as separate from discipleship, you need to rethink that idea. We will want to be sure that the "doing" of Christian living is built on a solid foundation of "knowing." You also will work to see that biblical and theological teaching really do contribute to the hearers' walk with Christ. The "teach" of the Great Commission is very specifically, "teach them *to obey* all things I have commanded you," rather than the teaching of information.

8. There is no discipleship without community.

The modern discipleship movement was birthed by para-church ministries that stressed particular methods of discipleship. Usually these methods revolved around a philosophy of multiplication that focused on small groups or one-to-one training. No doubt there is a great deal in this approach that has benefited Christian people, but this has also contributed to a highly individualistic understanding of discipleship. In fact, when discipleship is based on a faulty theology, there is even an assumption that most people in a church will *not* be interested in discipleship (often labeled the "carnal Christian"). Therefore, the assumption is that discipleship will be limited to just a few committed people.

However, once we understand discipleship in the broader sense of helping one another live our Christian lives, then the absolute necessity of the church community comes to the foreground. We are one Body in Christ and true growth comes as we grow up *together*.[23] God's appointed arena for making disciples is the church. The subtitle for Robert Webber's *Ancient-Future Evangelism* is *Making Your Church a Faith-Forming Community*. He writes, "Because the church is the reality of God made present, the church itself is a womb for disciple making."[24] He outlines how the early church formed new disciples—through immersion in the life of the church, through worship, through preaching, and through mentoring.[25] A pastor in North Carolina suggests the term, "organic discipleship" for the idea that our churches need to let the gospel unfold naturally in the context of our church life.[26]

It is also important to remember that a component of discipleship is *discipline*. It is the church, with the leadership of elders who are "shepherds of the flock," where the appropriate discipline of the disciple takes place. Timothy Witmer makes an important comment in this regard, "As a church leader the sheep *will* require your attention. It is your choice whether it will be the *reactive* care of running after the troubled and stray sheep or whether it will be time spent *proactively* caring for the sheep in a well-designed shepherding ministry."[27] Proactively guiding the sheep under the care of the elders is another way to describe a church-wide focus on making disciples.

Before attempting to design some kind of specific approach to discipleship for your unique situation, it is important to understand that the practical starting point in making disciples is what goes on in the ordinary weekly gatherings of the church for worship, teaching, and communion. This is where people learn their first lessons in prayer and in reading and understanding Scripture. The two sacraments—baptism and the Lord's Supper—are amazing tools to teach and demonstrate the realities of coming to faith and walking in faith. Think of the Sunday worship service as the hub whose spokes reach into every area of the life of the church. The traditional commitment of referring to the Word, sacraments, and prayer as the "ordinary means of grace"[28] needs to be brought into the foreground of discipleship if we have allowed them to be replaced by lesser means. The historic tools of discipleship, The Lord's Prayer, the Ten Commandments, and the Apostles' Creed are still basic building blocks that should be integral to helping those with little or no background grow up in the faith.[29] And learning to say them *together* will be part of that growth.

9. Discipleship begins with the next generation.

Perhaps the word *go* in the Great Commission causes people to first think of making disciples in terms of going somewhere and reaching those outside the church. In much of the discipleship literature the importance of reaching the next generation—the children born within the church—seems to receive only passing mention if discussed at all. This is a tragic omission. The *first* consideration in a church's mission to make disciples should be the discipleship of its own children. Pastors and other church leaders should feel the weight of Jesus' rebuke to his disciples when they thought he was too busy or too important to give serious attention to children who were brought to him (Matt. 19:13–15). Jesus blessed these children and made the extraordinary statement, "For to such belong the kingdom of heaven."[30] Peter made a point of telling his hearers on the Day of Pentecost that the gift of the Holy Spirit was for them "and for your children, and for all who are far off, everyone whom the Lord our God calls to himself" (Acts 2:39). Peter's statement, consistent with the teaching of the Old Testament, specifically included the next generation in those who were called. This means it is appropriate to visualize that among the 3000 lining up for baptism there would be parents bringing their children. Certainly children would have been included in the life of the new-born church: apostles' teaching, fellowship, breaking of bread and prayers, breaking bread in their homes, and praising God (Acts 2:42–47).

Those leading God's people are called to create an environment where parents who are committed to raise their children to follow Jesus are given all support possible. This may not mean more programs (in fact it may mean *fewer* programs so parents can have time to nurture their children), but any vision for making disciples must include the children. This includes helping parents understand the importance of spiritual training and offering practical guides for things like family worship. It will include a strategy for teaching children the essentials of the faith, possibly using the wonderful catechisms that were written for that purpose. It will include a strategy for preparing them to make a public profession of faith.[31] There are many good approaches to discipling the next generation, and this job must not be overlooked or treated with indifference. It is first priority in the call of Jesus to make disciples of all nations.

10. Following Jesus includes following Jesus in his mission.

From the very first words of his call, Jesus made it clear that his call to follow him as a disciple had a purpose—a mission. Not only was Jesus proclaiming and demonstrating the presence of the kingdom, he specifically told those he was calling that he would make them "fishers of men" (Mark 1:17). The men he was calling were fisherman so the phrase meant that their fundamental vocation would now be working with people instead of fish, and they would announce and demonstrate the gospel—the good news of the kingdom. It was necessary, in God's plan, that Jesus open the way for this mission by what he alone could do—his death, resurrection and ascension. Nevertheless, the ultimate mission was constantly before him throughout his earthly ministry (Luke 4:16–21, 43) and became his primary topic of teaching after his resurrection (Acts 1:3). We have already looked at the Great Commission, but consider also these words the risen Christ spoke to his assembled disciples the first time he met with them as a group: "As the Father has sent me, even so I am sending you" (John 20:21). The sense of this text is not only that Jesus now sends his disciples forth, but also that he sends them forth on the mission that was given to him by his Father.

The importance of Jesus' mission, which then became the mission of his church, is not a new issue.[32] However, it must be noted here that if this mission was part of Jesus' call from the beginning, then it needs to be part of our making disciples from the earliest steps in the process. Earlier in this booklet I mentioned the challenge of convincing believers that they are disciples; now the challenge becomes to convince these disciples that they are actually missionaries. Of course, the word *missionary* can bring various reactions, but at its most basic sense a missionary is someone on a mission, and a disciple of

Jesus is a person with a mission. One phrase that captures this sense of mission is "disciples making disciples."[33] This points to the fact that we are people still learning what it means to follow Jesus as his disciple, and we understand that an important part of that discipleship is helping those who may be a few steps behind us. Jesus told those first disciples that he would *make them* fishers of men. Jesus does this work as church leaders become Christ's instruments "to equip the saints for the work of ministry" (Eph. 4:12). And consider Paul's instruction to Timothy for the discipling of new leaders, "You then, my child, be strengthened by the grace that is in Christ Jesus, and what you have heard from me in the presence of many witnesses entrust to faithful men who will be able to teach others also" (2 Tim. 2:1, 2).

The mission and Jesus' challenge to be on that mission with him needs to be fully integrated into any approach a church takes to making disciples. As a practical matter this means that the outreach ministry of a church should be understood as a key ingredient of its overall discipleship ministry. Consider, for example, the value of short-term missions trips. Preparation for the trip and the prayer and teaching while on the trip should be viewed as making disciples on several levels. It will affect those who will be reached, but also those who are participating. This may be discipleship of those who are still young Christians or seeking. Why not invite a person who has yet to make a profession of faith along on a short-term missions trip if that person's skills could contribute to the purpose of the trip? If the purpose of the trip was to conduct a vacation Bible school or do street evangelism that would not be appropriate. But couldn't a nurse be invited to help with a clinic or a carpenter to help rebuild after an earthquake? I've met people who came to genuine faith on a church missions trip and whose whole outlook on the Christian walk was set in a context of ministry.

NEXT STEPS

The ten points just explained are intended as building blocks to lay a foundation for what ongoing discipleship could look like in your congregation. Now the real work begins. This could be a personal exercise, but I encourage you to find some others, or ask your leadership board to appoint others, who will join you in looking carefully at whether you think your church is a community that is making disciples. If the answer is no, or this is not something we do well, or we don't know, then begin to prayerfully outline how making disciples can move to the center of what your church is all about. If you are reading this as the leader of a ministry within your church—small group Bible study, youth, women, choir, or some other group—then begin to think about how your ministry could become more discipleship oriented. If you are a church planter, use this time to establish a congregation that knows from the outset that they are called to be a community of disciples.

If you are ready to move forward as a church that makes disciples, here are some steps you might follow:

· Agree on a basic statement of your goal that can become a focus for specific prayer. It is vital that you give serious attention to prayer that reflects a longing for an authentically Christ-centered, reproducing ministry. One example is, "We want to become a community of disciples of Jesus who are committed to growing in our own discipleship even as we make other disciples."
· Make sure you have a common vocabulary. Do you agree about the meaning of the words *disciple* and *discipleship*? Are your members in agreement that this is a matter of highest priority for your church?[34]

- Discuss together the ten steps in the list above. Make notes about what could be done in each of the areas I discussed. Do additional reading and assign people to study effective models of ministry.

- If you agree with my point that the ordinary, weekly gathering (usually the Sunday worship service) should be the hub from which discipleship spreads (point #8), ask yourselves how the Sunday service contributes (or doesn't contribute) to the discipleship of those who attend. For example, are people learning to read and understand the Bible? Are people learning how to pray? Are children growing because of the Sunday worship? Are unbelievers regularly coming and staying because they feel welcome and are drawn by what they hear from the pulpit?

- Before thinking about new programs, consider a larger vision of disciple-making that will permeate the whole life of the church and affect ministries that already exist. Recognize that training current ministry leaders to be more conscious of disciple-making is itself discipleship training. Once you have done that review there may still be a need to design a ministry specifically to help people move into a place of leadership as disciples who make disciples. The most effective programs I am aware of pull together many elements from other sources and ministries but are designed specifically by pastors and leaders for that particular congregation and its mission. Don't expect to find exactly what you think you need already packaged and ready to go.

- Take a fresh look at how you work with those preparing to join the church. This is a key time to introduce the core values of your ministry; joining a church is a "teachable moment" for most people. Do you have a plan to take these new members on to greater maturity in Christ? This is the time to introduce that plan as part of the normal participation of those who are members of your church.

· What about the nurture of your children? Have you applied these thoughts about making disciples to the way the children of the congregation are being helped? Sunday school will be one element of their discipleship, but think about what else this includes.

· Identify some small but specific steps that you can take to begin to reorient your congregation (or strengthen a commitment you already have) to a greater vision for making disciples. The long-term goal should be a plan that will shape the whole church, but that kind of change comes slowly to most congregations. It is better to take small steps than develop a grand plan that never becomes practical.

Dr. C. John (Jack) Miller wrote *Outgrowing the Ingrown Church* for those he called "pacesetters." He challenged them to take a new look at the call of the Great Commission and the need for leaders to lead their churches in obedience to the clear mandate of Jesus. Jack used his own life and repentance as an example and told the story of founding a new church and church movement that came about as a result of his own transformation. I pray that his words speak to your heart and encourage you to move by faith to hear and obey the command of Jesus.

So let me call you and your congregation, not simply to survival for another week, but to radical commitment: to believe Christ's promises and to do His will at all costs. That will is revealed in His command to the church to go with the gospel to the nations and make disciples of them. Our task, then, is a missionary task. This mission consists in the whole outreach enterprise of evangelizing and discipling mankind, and it involves the participation of every living member of the local congregation.[35]

NOTES

1. For example, a recent search on Amazon.com brought up 8500 responses to the word "discipleship."
2. Colin Marshall and Tony Payne, *The Trellis and the Vine* (Kingsford, Australia: Matthias Media, 2009), 13–14. Written by people of Reformed conviction, this book is an excellent resource for the challenge of building disciple-making churches. It also introduces Matthias Media (www.matthiasmedia.com), producer of helpful discipleship material for 25 years.
3. Ibid., 8.
4. Ibid., 9.
5. Glenn McDonald, *The Disciple Making Church* (Grand Haven, MI: Faith-Walk Publishing, 2007), 4.
6. James Montgomery Boice, *Christ's Call to Discipleship* (Chicago: Moody Press, 1986), 16.
7. The comments of Dietrich Bonhoeffer on this passage are particularly insightful. See chap. 2, "The Call to Discipleship" in *The Cost of Discipleship* (New York: Touchstone Books, 1995 ed.).
8. Stephen Smallman, *The Walk* (Phillipsburg, NJ: P&R Publishers, 2009), 26.
9. See pp. 23-28 of Stephen E. Smallman, *Spiritual Birthline: Understanding How We Experience the New Birth* (Wheaton: Crossway Books, 2006). This is my effort to define terms and explain the new birth using the paradigm of physical birth. Chap. 5 of *The Walk* also includes the "birthline."
10. Question #31, Westminster Shorter Catechism.
11. Walter A. Henrichsen, *Disciples Are Made Not Born* (Wheaton: Victor Books, 1974; Wheaton: David C. Cook, 2002).
12. Robert E. Webber, *Ancient-Future Evangelism: Making Your Church a Faith-Forming Community* (Grand Rapids, MI: Baker Books, 2003).
13. This is the core of World Harvest Mission's renewal ministry. Check its website for resources: www.whm.org. Two other examples are C.J. Mahaney, *Living the Cross Centered Life* (Colorado Springs, CO: Multnomah

Books, 2006) and Milton Vincent, *A Gospel Primer for Christians* (Newburyport, MA: Focus Publishing, 2008).

14. Jerry Bridges, *The Discipline of Grace* (Colorado Springs, CO: NavPress, 1994), 19-21.

15. Archibald Alexander, *Thoughts on Religious Experience* (London: Banner of Truth Trust, 1967 ed, first published in 1844), 165–66.

16. This is a phrase that captures the essence of the call for renewal by church historian Richard Lovelace. His book, *Dynamics of Spiritual Life: An Evangelical Theology of Renewal* (Madison, WI: Inter-Varsity Press, 1979), is one of the seminal influences in the modern reawakening to the centrality of the gospel.

17. Michael Horton, *The Gospel-Driven Life* (Grand Rapids, MI: Baker Books, 2009), 77.

18. Step One: Know the gospel itself; Step Two: Know how you came to believe the gospel; Step Three: Know the benefits of believing the gospel (gospel doctrine); Step Four: Live a life that flows from the gospel (gospel obedience). Smallman, *The Walk*, chaps. 4-11.

19. Colossians 1:9 (know), 1:10 (that you may live/walk/do).

20. Horton, *The Gospel-Driven Life*, 98–99.

21. Ephesians 1:15-19; 3:14-19; Philippians 3:7-11.

22. Horton, *The Gospel-Driven Life*, 150.

23. Ephesians 4:11-16.

24. Webber, *Ancient-Future Evangelism*, 74.

25. Ibid., 73-85.

26. Winfield Bevins, *Grow: Reproducing through Organic Discipleship* (available online at: http://theresurgence.com/files/grow6x9moderate-A.pdf), 11.

27. Timothy Z. Witmer, *The Shepherd Leader* (Phillipsburg, NJ: P&R Publishing, 2010), 249.

28. Question #88, Westminster Shorter Catechism.

29. Note that the Heidelberg Catechism (1563), one of the earliest Reformed discipling resources, is formed around these three pillars.

30. While this text doesn't explicitly teach the baptism of infants and children, it certainly supports the validity of bringing children to Jesus in a public setting for his blessing. See my booklet, "How Our Children Come to Faith" (Phillipsburg, NJ: P&R Publishing, 2006). This was written as a pastoral booklet to be given to new parents.

31. See Stephen Smallman, *Understanding the Faith: A Workbook for Communicants Classes and Others Preparing to Make a Public Profession of Faith* (Phillipsburg, NJ: P&R Publishing, rev. ed., 2009).
32. However the centrality of the kingdom of God in the understanding of that mission has been a matter of great discussion. Two helpful introductions are Charles Dunahoo, *Making Kingdom Disciples* (Phillipsburg, NJ: P&R Publishing, 2005), Tullian Tchividjian, *Unfashionable* (Colorado Springs, CO: Multnomah Books, 2009).
33. Smallman,*The Walk*, chap. 12.
34. The subtitle of *The Trellis and the Vine* is "The ministry mind-shift that changes everything." That is what most of us need. Note chap. 2 for an outline of what this mind-shift looks like.
35. C. John Miller, *Outgrowing the Ingrown Church* (Grand Rapids, MI: Zondervan Publishing House, 1986), 25.